# A PICTURE TOUR OF

SMITHSONIAN INSTITUTION PRESS, WASHINGTON, D.C.

# THE SMITHSONIAN

The Smithsonian Institution brings to life the nation's cultural, social, scientific, and artistic treasures and heritage. It is the largest complex of museums, art galleries, and research facilities in the world. Each year, the Smithsonian's 13 museums and galleries and the National Zoological Park record more than 26 million visitors. Millions more share in the Smithsonian experience through traveling exhibitions land; the National Zoo's animal conservation and research center near Front Royal, Virginia; a tropical research center and natural preserve in the Republic of Panama; an environmental research center with facilities in Edgewater, Maryland; a marine station at Fort Pierce, Florida; and astrophysical stations in Cambridge, Massachusetts, and on Mount Hopkins near Tucson, Arizona.

Smithsonian research, now well into its second century, is

# WELCOME TO THE SMITHSONIAN

displayed across the United States and abroad, through *Smithsonian* and *Air & Space/Smithsonian* magazines, as members of the Smithsonian Associates, and by attendance at educational and performance programs sponsored by the Institution, including the annual Festival of American Folklife on the National Mall.

Visitors come to trace the landmarks of flight, to marvel at the complexity of life on this planet, to gain insight into our nation's history and the men and women who shaped it, to contemplate the works of artists and craftspeople from ancient times to the present day. And while the visitors explore the galleries and exhibition halls, a multitude of curators, conservators, and researchers are busy behind the scenes caring for and learning from the national collections that the Smithsonian holds in trust for the American people.

The collections, which now number more than 137 million objects, continue to grow at a rate of about half a million scientific specimens, works of art, and cultural artifacts a year. Most of these new objects become part of the study collections, for only a tiny percentage of the Smithsonian collections is on display in the museums at any one time.

Visitors to the Smithsonian museums are often unaware of the wide array of research conducted behind the scenes by the Institution's curatorial and research staff. Extensive research programs, in fields as varied as paleobiology, desertification, and American art, are carried out in the individual museums. In addition, the Smithsonian has a number of special research facilities. They include a facility for the preservation, restoration, and storage of air- and spacecraft in Suitland, Maryland; the National Zoo's animal conservation and research center near Front Royal, Virginia; a tropical research center and natural preserve in the Republic of Panama; an environmental research center with facilities in Edgewater, Maryland; a marine station at Fort Pierce, Florida; and astrophysical stations in Cambridge, Massachusetts, and on Mount Hopkins near Tucson, Arizona.

still fresh and exciting. Smithsonian historians at the Archives of American Art search the length and breadth of the nation for documents relating to all aspects of American art history. Smithsonian curators and scholarly staff have taken their quest for knowledge to every continent and major group of islands in the world and to worlds beyond our own. With support from public and private sources, Smithsonian researchers have a tradition of seeking new knowledge and exploring new intellectual and physical frontiers.

The Smithsonian Institution was born from the generous legacy of James Smithson, a wealthy English scientist. It was created by an act of Congress in 1846 to carry out the terms of Smithson's will, which bequeathed his entire estate to the United States of America "to found at Washington, under the name of the Smithsonian Institution, an establishment for the increase and diffusion of knowledge." In the past century and a half since its establishment, the Smithsonian has evolved into the world's largest cultural and scientific complex.

*Opposite:* Shang dynasty ritual wine container, 15th century B.C., Arthur M. Sackler Gallery; woman and child figure made by the Yombe of Zaire, National Museum of African Art. *Preceding pages: Page 1.* The heraldic lion of the Smithsonian Mace, a symbol of the Smithsonian Institution, holds a sunburst signifying the power of knowledge. *Pages 2-3.* Sunset silhouettes the Smithsonian Institution Building, popularly known as the Castle.

Housing more than 17 million objects, the National Museum of American History illuminates U.S. history in all its breadth. The museum displays artifacts that encompass America's social and cultural history, from its domestic and community life to its performing and applied arts. Objects related to science and technology document American contribu-tions to agriculture, transportation, manufacturing, medicine, printing, computing, and other industries and professions. Extensive stamp and coin collections are also included. The Dibner Library of rare books and the Archives Center further extend the museum's offerings. ***Preceding pages:*** The *John Bull*, built in England and shipped to New Jersey in 1831, was one of the first railway engines

# NATIONAL MUSEUM OF AMERICAN HISTORY

1

2

3

4

5

in the United States; today it is the world's oldest working locomotive. *1.* The historic Star-Spangled Banner flew over Fort McHenry during the War of 1812 and inspired the Francis Scott Key poem that became our national anthem. *2.* This red velocipede of 1869 represents a typical early example of pedal power. *3.* Leon Scott's phonautograph, built in 1857, was the first machine to record sound. *4.* This early commercial telegraph key was designed for Samuel F. B. Morse by his associate Alfred Vail about 1845. *5.* This Bible quilt, created in the 1880s by Harriet Powers, a black woman born in slavery, is an important example of American quiltmaking and design. *6.* Teddy Bear was named in honor of U.S. president Theodore Roosevelt. *7.* The first Xerox machine was invented in the late 1930s. *8.* George Washington's sword is the second from the right in this display. *9.* Thomas Jefferson drafted the Declaration of Independence at this lap writing desk, which he designed.

6

7

8

9

10

11

12

13

14

*10. St. Anthony of Padua* was painted by a Franciscan friar on tanned hide in Spanish New Mexico about 1725. *11.* The Franklin 5-cent and Washington 10-cent stamps of 1847 were the first U.S. postage stamps issued for general service throughout the nation. *12.* With its inverted center, this 24-cent airmail stamp is one of America's rarest philatelic collectors' items. *13.* George Washington used this field tent during the American Revolution. *14.* A mannequin models Barbara Bush's inaugural gown in the popular Ceremonial Court.

*15.* Benjamin Franklin may have worked as a printer's journeyman on this wooden press in London about 1726. *16.* These election buttons are a few of the thousands in the museum's collections. *17.* This Bessemer-style converter, invented in the 1850s, was used in U.S. experiments to manufacture steel from pig iron. *18.* The Foucault pendulum provides a visual demonstration of the earth's rotation. *19.* This is a reproduction of the astronomical clock Giovanni de'Dondi of Padua, Italy, built around 1350.

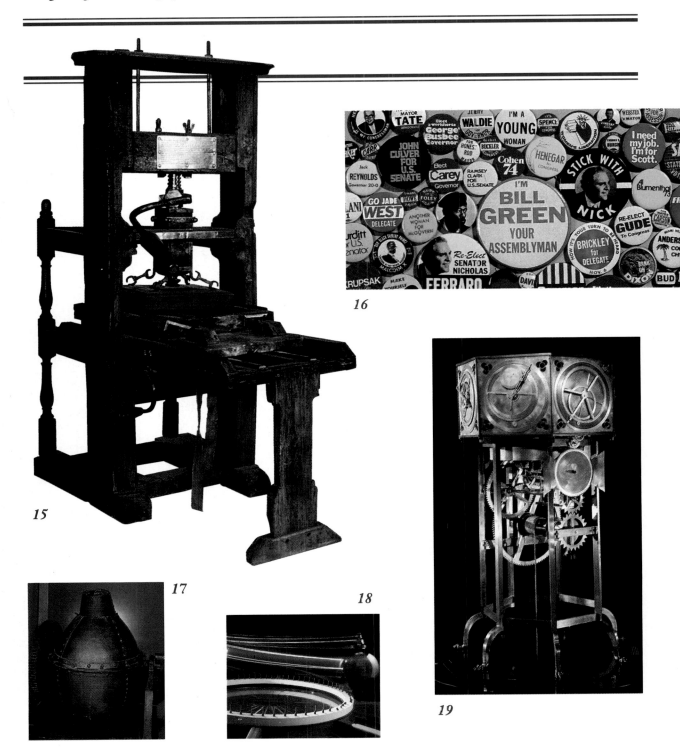

15

16

17

18

19

20. In northern sections of the United States, one-man sleds like this were widely used at the turn of the century to deliver Rural Free Delivery mail. 21. Fashioned by a contemporary Seneca Indian doll maker, these corn husk dolls wear ceremonial dress typical of Iroquois peoples of the 1700s. 22. This banjo was manufactured in 1860 by Fred Mather of New York. 23. This sharecropper's kitchen display is from the "Field to Factory" exhibit. 24. Pewter objects like these were widely used in 18th- and early 19th-century America.

25. A creation of Faith Bradford, this dollhouse depicts an idealized view of a large and affluent American family of the early 1900s. 26. Earthenware and stoneware vessels like these were common in American households of the late 18th century. 27. The Dunham schoolroom, brought to the museum from Cleveland, Ohio, is re-created as it might have looked in 1915. 28. The Conestoga wagon was developed in Pennsylvania in the late 18th century.

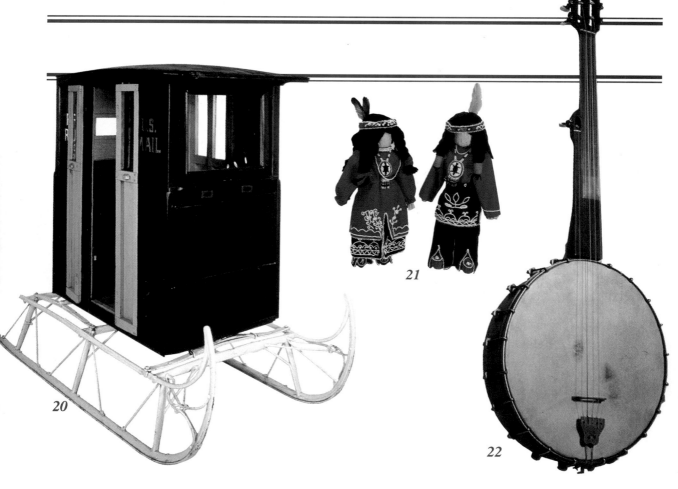

21

20

22

23

24

25

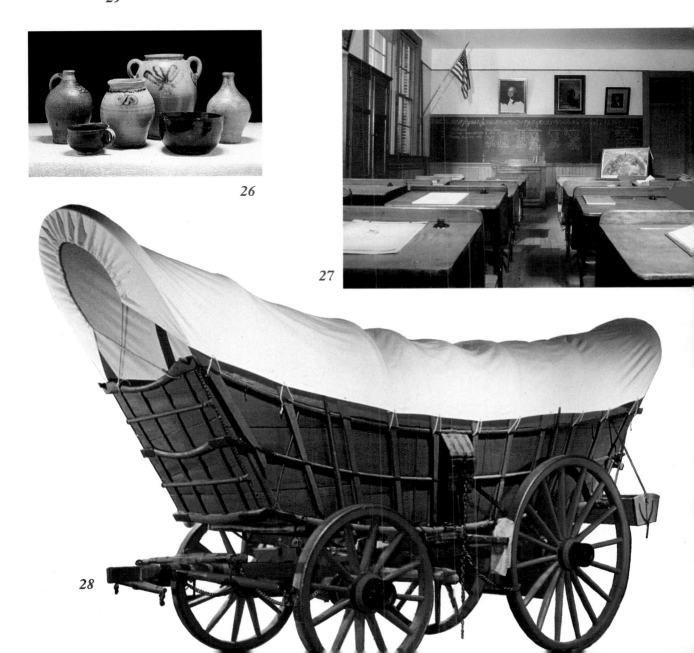

26

27

28

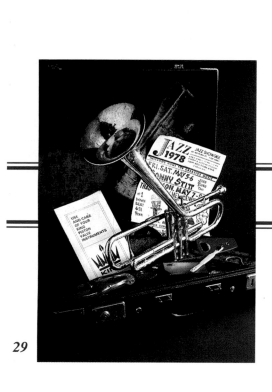

29

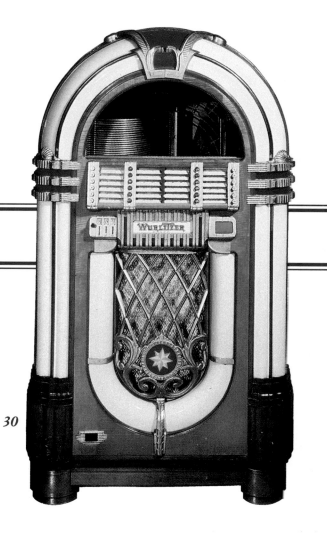

30

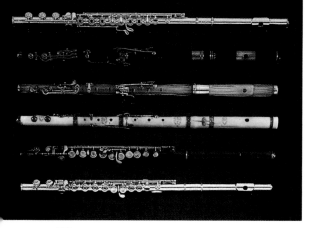

31

32

33

29. Jazz great John "Dizzy" Gillespie used this King "Silver Flair" trumpet. 30. This Wurlitzer jukebox cranked out hits in the late 1940s. 31. These flutes are made from materials ranging from glass to gold. 32. Dorothy wore these magical ruby slippers in the American film classic *The Wizard of Oz.* 33. The Swamp Rat XXX, a top-fuel dragster, was designed and built by Don Garlits in 1986. 34. This $50 bill was part of the first $1 million issued by the Confederacy in 1861. 35. This $20 gold coin is a beautiful example of the museum's vast coin collection. 36. The John Deere Model D tractor was manufactured from 1924 to 1953.

34

35

36

The Arts and Industries Building is the second oldest Smithsonian building on the Mall. Three of its four halls display objects from the 1876 United States International Exhibition, held in Philadelphia. The exhibition was opened in honor of the country's Bicentennial in 1976 and is a re-creation of the centennial exhibit. Steam-powered machines, examples of the decorative arts, all types of manufactured goods, and much more can be seen. The high Victorian building was designed by Adolph Cluss from a floor plan by Montgomery C. Meigs. Completed in 1881, it was the first building built specifically as a museum and designed for maximum light and good visitor flow. In 1991 an Experimental Gallery will be created in the

# ARTS AND INDUSTRIES BUILDING

1

2

3

fourth hall, with opportunities for exploring exhibition theories and techniques in the sciences, humanities, and the arts of many cultures. *1.* A flag-bedecked sign re-creates the spirit of the 1876 Centennial Exhibition. *2.* The magnificent rotunda ceiling commands attention. *3.* The exuberant facade of the Arts and Industries Building reflects the eclectic architectural tastes of the Victorian era. *4.* This elaborate display shows the wares of the E. Butterick Co., one of the pioneer manufacturers of sewing patterns in America. *5.* Jerome B. Rice & Co.'s flower seeds and their packages are highlighted in this arrangement. *6.* Built in 1876 by the Baldwin Locomotive Works, the *Jupiter* was originally engine No. 3 for the Santa Cruz Railroad.

4

5

A dazzling array of flying machines and spacecraft awaits visitors to the National Air and Space Museum. Approximately nine million people visit the museum annually, making it the world's most popular museum. The museum's 23 exhibition areas include dozens of airplanes and spacecraft, missiles and rockets, engines, propellers, models, uniforms, instruments, flight equipment, medals, and insignia. These items document most of the major achievements, both historical and technological, of air and space flight. Throughout the day the museum presents films on flight and planetarium shows. *Preceding pages:* Detail from *The Space Mural — A Cosmic View* by Robert McCall. This striking 75-foot-wide mural greets visitors entering the museum from Independence Avenue

# NATIONAL AIR AND SPACE MUSEUM

1

2

4

3

(© Robert McCall; NASM photo). *1.* Orville Wright made the first manned, powered, heavier-than-air flight in the *Flyer* at Kitty Hawk, North Carolina, on December 17, 1903. *2.* The Ford Trimotor, "The Tin Goose" (front), was a reliable passenger plane of the 1920s and 1930s. The Douglas D-3 is shown behind. *3.* The Fokker T-2, an Army Air Service transport, was the first to fly nonstop from coast to coast in 1923. *4.* Two French noblemen made the first flight into the atmosphere (3,000 feet up) on November 21, 1783, over Versailles, France, in the Montgolfier brothers' hot-air balloon, shown in this model. *5.* Charles Lindbergh made the first solo transatlantic flight in the Ryan NYP, *Spirit of St. Louis,* in May 1927. The flight, from New York to Paris, took 33½ hours. *6.* Amelia Earhart made history as the first woman to fly solo across the Atlantic in May 1932 in this Lockheed 5B Vega. *7.* The Douglas M-2 was an airmail aircraft of the 1920s.

6

5

8

9

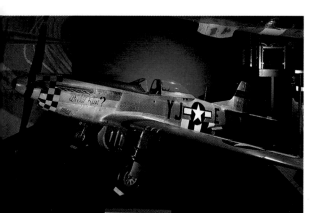

10

11

8. The Spitfire is one of the classic aircraft of all time and one of Britain's most important in World War II. This Mark VII is one of the 20,000 built in more than 40 versions. 9. Wiley Post's Lockheed 5C Vega, *Winnie Mae*, was the first plane to fly solo around the world, July 15–22, 1933. 10. North American P-51, the Mustang, was a highly successful American fighter of the second half of World War II. 11. The Lockheed F-104 Starfighter can fly at twice the speed of sound. 12. First introduced in 1940, the Mitsubishi Zero, a carrier-based fighter, was the outstanding Japanese aircraft of World War II. 13. The Messerschmitt Bf 109, first produced in 1937, was one of Germany's standard single-seat fighter planes. 14. The Douglas SBD Dauntless, a U.S. Navy dive bomber, played the key role in the Battle of Midway, sinking four Japanese aircraft carriers.

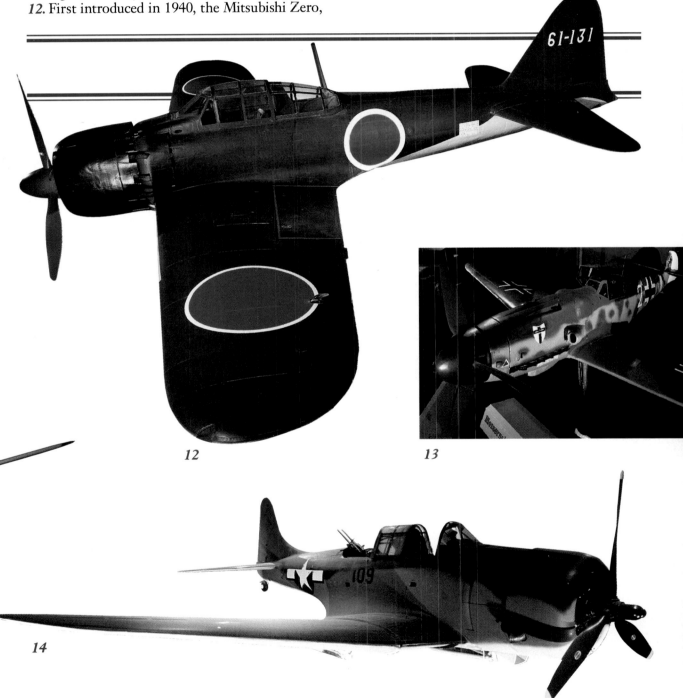

12

13

14

**15.** The rocket-powered North American X-15, first flown in 1959, reached maximum speeds in excess of 4,500 mph and reached heights of over 67 miles, bridging the gap between air and space flight. **16.** Mastering the theories of rocket physics, liquid fuel propulsion, and gyrostabilization, Robert H. Goddard built these rockets. **17.** The Soviet Union launched *Sputnik 1*, shown in this replica of the world's first successful satellite, on October 4, 1957. **18.** Chuck Yeager's Bell X-1 was the first American rocket-powered aircraft and the first aircraft to break the speed of sound (700 mph or Mach 1.06) on October 14, 1947. **19.** Space Hall displays a panorama of rockets, satellites, and probes. **20.** The *Voyager*, the first aircraft to fly nonstop around the world without refueling, began and ended its flight at Edwards Air Force Base in California. Pilots Jeana Yeager and Dick Rutan completed the 9-day, 3-minute, and 44-second flight on December 23, 1986. **21.** This *Explorer I* backup depicts America's first successful satellite, launched on January 31, 1958.

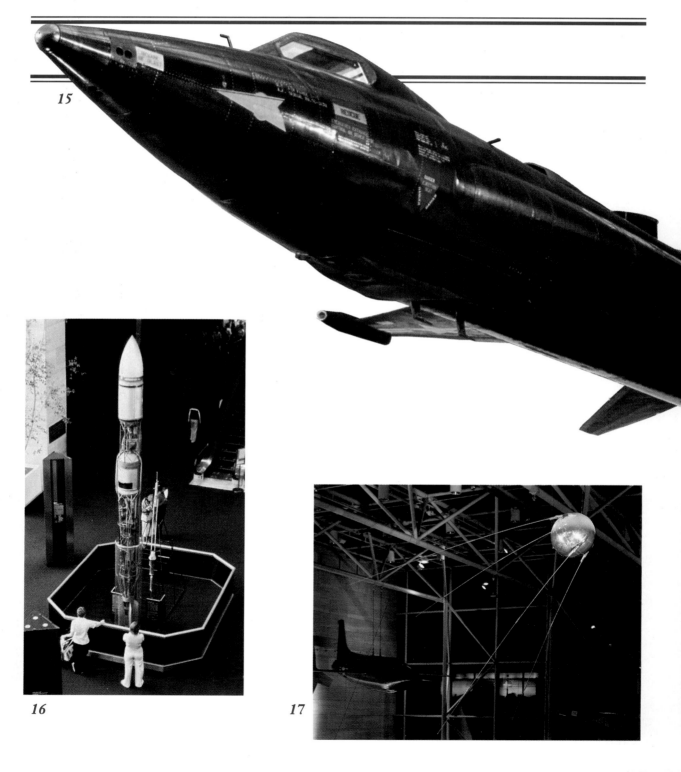

15

16

17

*18*

*19*

*20*

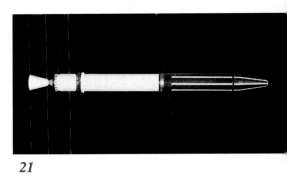

*21*

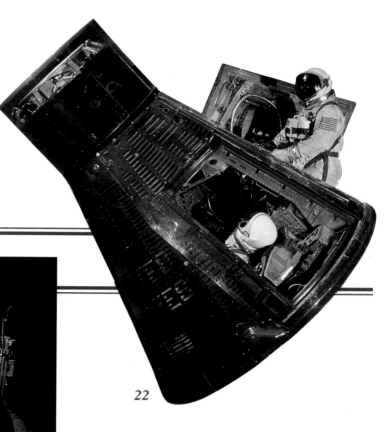

22

23

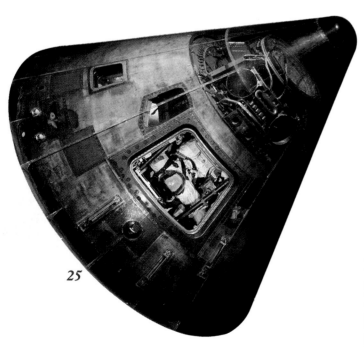

25

24

26

**22.** From the *Gemini 4,* astronaut Edward H. White became the first American to "walk in space." **23.** This Lunar Roving Vehicle is similar to those used to explore the moon in the Apollo program. **24.** In the background of this lunar module display is the U.S. Capitol. **25.** The *Apollo 11* command module served as the "base station" for Neil Armstrong, Edwin "Buzz" Aldrin, and Michael Collins on their historic journey to the moon. **26.** Visitors can go "on board" Skylab. **27.** Two unmanned Viking Landers, like this engineering replica, landed on Mars in 1976 and sent back important scientific data on the planet. **28.** An astronaut model poses aboard Skylab, the first U.S. space station. **29.** The Space Shuttle Orbiter *Enterprise,* now in the National Air and Space Museum collection, is shown here being ferried aboard a NASA 747.

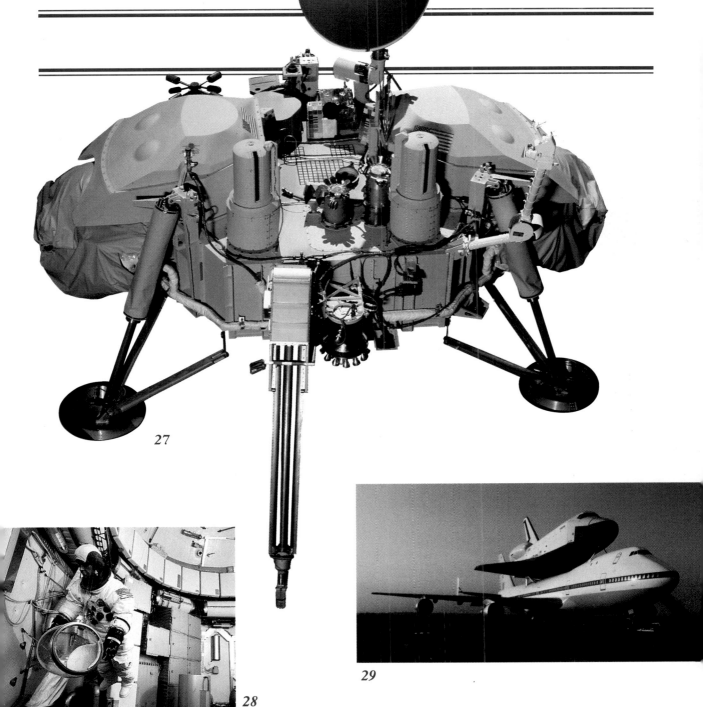

27

28

29

The National Museum of African Art is the only U.S. museum devoted to collecting, exhibiting, and studying the visual arts of Africa south of the Sahara. The museum, which moved to the National Mall in 1987, features the finest examples of African sculpture, textiles, household objects, architectural elements, musical instruments, and decorative arts. The galleries ex- hibit art from the permanent collection of 6,000 works on a rotating basis, as well as special exhibitions on loan from public and private institutions. The museum houses the Warren M. Robbins Library of 20,000 books and the Eliot Elisofon Archives, which maintains more than 200,000 images of African art and culture. *1.* Muzamba-style mask *(pwo)*, Chokwe peoples, Zaire and Angola, wood, fiber, and metal.

# NATIONAL MUSEUM OF AFRICAN ART

1

2

3

**2.** Harp, Zande peoples, Zaire, wood, animal hide, and metal. **3.** Headrest, Luba peoples, Zaire, wood. **4.** Staff with a female figure and child *(oshe Shango)*, Yoruba peoples, Nigeria, wood, pigment, and glass beads. **5.** Memorial grave figure of a colonial officer, Bamum peoples, Cameroon, wood, brass, glass beads, and

cowrie shells; gift of Evelyn A. J. Hall and John A. Friede. **6.** Commemorative cast copper alloy head with iron inlays, Benin, Nigeria, 15th or 16th century. **7.** Figure of a seated male and female *(Akua'ba)*, Asante group, Akan peoples, Ghana, wood and pigment.

4

5

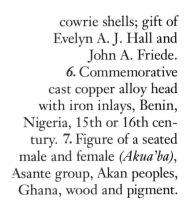

6

7

One of the world's finest collections of Asian art is in the Freer Gallery of Art. The choice selection of more than 26,000 art objects spanning six millennia shows the variety and sophistication of cultures from Japan to the Mediterranean. Also of note are the James McNeill Whistler collections — the largest in the United States — and works by a circle of American artists ac-

tive in the late 19th and early 20th centuries whose art shows a sensitivity to and compatibility with Asian arts. The gift of Charles Lang Freer, the gallery was opened to the public in 1923 and was the first Smithsonian museum built exclusively to house the fine arts. The Freer Gallery is closed for renovation until 1992. *1. Mount Fuji,* Japanese painting by Katsushika Hokusai (1760–1849), Ukiyo-e school, Edo period,

# FREER GALLERY OF ART

1

2

3

4

5

19th century. *2.* Japanese lacquer cabinet, Momoyama or early Edo period, early 17th century. *3.* Japanese pottery incense case, attributed to Ninsei, Edo period, mid-17th century. *4.* Japanese fan painting by Ogata Kōrin (circa 1658–1716), Rimpa school, Edo period, 17th to 18th century. *5.* Chinese dry lacquer Buddhist sculpture of a Bodhisattva, Yüan dynasty, 13th century. *6.* Detail of a Japanese painting by Yosa Buson (1716–1784) of myna birds in a plum tree, 1776. *7.* Persian pottery, Samanid period, 10th century. *8.* Chinese Fa-hua-type jar with colored glazes, Ming dynasty, circa 1500. *9.* Peacock Room, James McNeill Whistler (1834–1903), oil, color, and gold on leather and wood. *10.* Chinese bronze ceremonial vessel of the type *he*, Shang dynasty, 11th century B.C.

6

7

8

9

10

The Arthur M. Sackler Gallery, the Smithsonian's newest museum, displays the fascinating breadth of artistic production in Asia from ancient times to the present through a lively schedule of international exhibitions and interpretive programs that complement the permanent collection. The basis of the museum is a gift of approximately 1,000 art objects, including Chinese bronzes, jades, paintings, and lacquerware; ancient Near Eastern silver and gold; and stone and bronze sculpture from South and Southeast Asia given by the late medical researcher, publisher, and art collector Dr. Arthur M. Sackler. Of special interest are scrolls by important 20th-century Chinese painters, a stunning jade collection, and an unparalleled set of Islamic and Persian painting and manuscripts, made by pigments

# ARTHUR M. SACKLER GALLERY

1

2

3

4

ground from malachite, lapis lazuli, gold, silver, and vermilion. The Gallery is housed in an innovative underground building on the National Mall, part of the Smithsonian's new quadrangle complex. *1.* Chinese bronze ritual wine vessel, 13th century B.C. *2.* Chinese carved red dish, Yüan dynasty, 13th to 14th centuries, lacquer on wood. *3. A Demon Descends upon a Horseman*, from a copy of the *Falnama*, ascribed to Ja'far al-Sadiq, Iran, circa 1550, opaque watercolor and gold on paper. *4.* Silver and gilt rhyton, probably Iran, 5th to 6th century. *5.* Chinese painting *Wild Geese, Sand Bar*, Sheng Maoye (circa 1607–1637), Ming dynasty. *6.* Detail of Chinese hanging scroll *Lotus*, Qi Baishi (1863–1957), ink and color on paper. *7.* Seated South Indian goddess, Chola dynasty, 10th century, granite. *8.* Chinese bronze ritual vessel, *zun*, Western Zhou dynasty, 10th century B.C.

5

6

7

8

The National Portrait Gallery houses more than 14,000 portraits of men and women who have made significant contributions to the history, development, and culture of the United States. The portraits displayed are in various media — paintings, sculptures, drawings, and photographs. Of special interest are the Hall of Presidents, decorated in the style of the mid-19th century, where portraits of all the chief executives can be found; the Gallery of Notable Americans; and the portraits chronicling the Civil War. The National Portrait Gallery shares space in the Old Patent Office Building with the National Museum of American Art. (Unless otherwise noted, all paintings are oil on canvas and all artists American.)

*1. Self-portrait*, 1780–1784, by John Singleton

# NATIONAL PORTRAIT GALLERY

*1*

Ætatis suæ 21. Aᵒ. 1616.

Matoaks als Rebecka daughter to the mighty Prince Powhatan Emperour of Attanoughkomouck als Virginia converted and baptized in the Christian faith, and Wife to the woro Mr Tho: Rolff.

*2*

*3*

Copley (1738–1815), gift of the Morris and Gwendolyn Cafritz Foundation and matching funds from the Smithsonian Institution. *2. Pocahontas*, post-1616, by unidentified artist after Simon van de Passe, transfer from the National Gallery of Art, gift of Andrew W. Mellon, 1942. *3. Benjamin Franklin*, circa 1785, by Joseph Siffred Duplessis (French, 1725–1802), gift of the Morris and Gwendolyn Cafritz Foundation. *4. Abraham Lincoln*, 1865, photograph, albumen silver print by Alexander Gardner (Scottish, 1821–1882). *5. Frederick Douglass*, 1856, ambrotype by unidentified photographer, gift of an anonymous donor. *6. Mary Cassatt*, circa 1880–1884, by Edgar Degas (French, 1834–1917), gift of the Morris and Gwendolyn Cafritz Foundation and the Regents' Major Acquisitions Fund, Smithsonian Institution. *7. Henry James*, 1911, charcoal on paper by Cecilia Beaux (1855–1942).

4

5

6

7

8

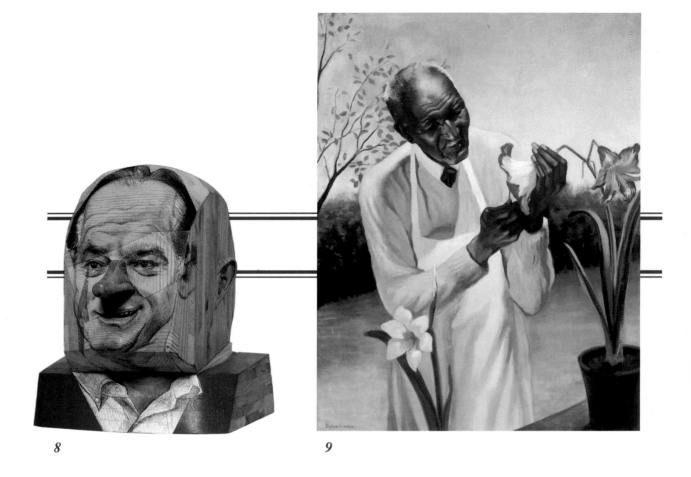

9

10

11

*8. Bob Hope*, 1967, polychromed wood by Marisol (b. 1930), gift of Time Inc. *9. George Washington Carver*, 1942, by Betsy Graves Reyneau (1888–1964), transfer from the National Museum of American Art, gift of the George Washington Carver Memorial Committee to the Smithsonian Institution, 1944. *10. Gertrude Stein*, 1922–1923, terra-cotta by Jo Davidson (1883–1952), gift of Dr. Maury Leibovitz. *11. Franklin Delano Roosevelt*, 1945, by Douglas Chandor (British, 1897–1953). *12. Joe Louis*, 1946, by Betsy Graves Rey-neau (1888–1964), gift of the Harmon Foundation. *13. Self-portrait with Rita*, 1922, by Thomas Hart Benton (1889–1975), gift of Mr. and Mrs. Jack H. Mooney. *14. Isamu Noguchi*, 1984 print from 1983 negative, photograph, gelatin silver print by Irving Penn (b. 1917), gift of Irving Penn.

12

13

14

Surveying 200 years of American art, the National Museum of American Art has more than 34,000 paintings, sculptures, folk art pieces, graphics, and photographs in its collection. Of special interest are major holdings of works by Albert Pinkham Ryder, George Catlin, Hiram Powers, miniature portraitists, 19th-century landscape painters and impressionists, and the artists of the Depression era. Post–World War II paintings and sculptures are installed in the magnificent Lincoln Gallery. The museum shares the historic Old Patent Office Building with the National Portrait Gallery. (Unless otherwise noted, all paintings are oil on canvas and all artists are American.) *1.* George Catlin (1796–1872), *Buffalo Bull's Back Fat, head chief, Blood tribe,* 1832, gift of

# NATIONAL MUSEUM OF AMERICAN ART

1

2

3

4

Mrs. Joseph Harrison, Jr. 2. Thomas Moran (1837–1926), *Cliffs of the Upper Colorado River, Wyoming Territory*, 1882, bequest of Henry Ward Ranger through the National Academy of Design. 3. Winslow Homer (1836–1910), *High Cliff, Coast of Maine*, 1894, gift of William T. Evans. 4. Mary Cassatt (1844–1926), *The Caress*, 1902, gift of William T. Evans. 5. Albert Pinkham Ryder (1847–1917), *The Flying Dutchman*, circa 1887, gift of John Gellatly. 6. Albert Bierstadt (1830–1902), *Among the Sierra Nevada Mountains, California*, 1868, bequest of Helen Huntington Hull.

5

6

7

8

9

7. William H. Johnson (1901–1970), *Man in a Vest*, 1939–1940, gift of Harmon Foundation. 8. Edward Hopper (1882–1967), *Cape Cod Morning*, 1950, gift of Sara Roby Foundation. 9. Paul Manship (1885–1966), *Diana*, 1925, bronze, gift of artist. 10. Yasuo Kuniyoshi (b. Japan, 1893–1953), *Strong Woman and Child*, 1925, gift of Sara Roby Foundation. 11. Louis Simon (b. Russia, 1884–1970), *Bicycle Shop Sign*, circa early 1930s, carved and painted wood with metal, rubber, and glass marbles, gift of Herbert Waide Hemphill, Jr., and museum purchase made possible by Ralph Cross Johnson. 12. Thomas Hart Benton (1889–1975), *Achelous and Hercules*, 1947, tempera and oil on canvas, gift of Allied Stores Corporation and museum purchase.

10

11

12

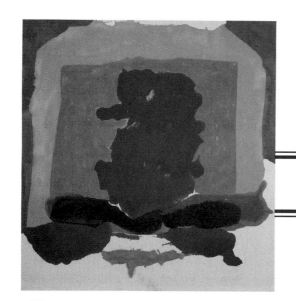

13

14

*13.* Helen Frankenthaler (b. 1928), *Small's Paradise*, 1964, acrylic on canvas, gift of George L. Erion. *14.* Franz Kline (1910–1962), untitled, 1961, acrylic on canvas, museum purchase from the Vincent Melzac Collection. *15.* Jacob Lawrence (b. 1917), *The Library*, 1960, tempera on fiberboard, gift of S. C. Johnson & Son, Inc.

15

The Renwick Gallery, a department of the National Museum of American Art, collects and exhibits American crafts. Built during the Civil War era, it was the first art museum in Washington, D.C., the original Corcoran Gallery of Art, and was later renamed for its architect, James Renwick. The museum presents changing exhibitions of contemporary American crafts as well as a selection of objects, dating from 1900 to the present, from its permanent collection. *1.* Portal gates, Albert Paley, installed in the Renwick Gallery in 1976, hand-forged, hot rolled steel and brass. *2.* The Grand Salon, restored in the opulent style of the 1870s, is among Washington's most handsome Victorian interiors. *3. Oval Chamber,* William Daley, 1986, stoneware, gift of the James Renwick Alliance and museum purchase.

# RENWICK GALLERY

1

2

3

The Hirshhorn Museum and Sculpture Garden is the Smithsonian's showcase for modern and contemporary art. Its collection ranges from portraits and landscapes of the late 19th century to outsize canvases and sculptures of the present day. Displaying and acquiring works by living artists are important roles for the museum, as it collects and preserves the art of our time. With 900 pieces of art on display in the museum and adjacent garden, the museum attracts more than one million visitors a year. The gift of Joseph H. Hirshhorn, the unusual drum-shaped building is uniquely designed for displaying modern art and almost appears to be a sculpture itself. (Unless otherwise noted, all works are gifts of Joseph H. Hirshhorn, the Joseph H. Hirshhorn Purchase Fund, or the Joseph H. Hirshhorn Foundation; paintings are oil on canvas if no

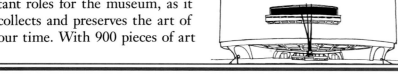

# HIRSHHORN MUSEUM AND SCULPTURE GARDEN

1

2

3

4

medium is specified.) *1.* Edward Hopper (American, 1882–1967), *Eleven A. M.*, 1926. *2.* Thomas Eakins (American, 1844–1916), *Frank B. A. Linton*, 1904. *3.* Mary Cassatt (American, 1844–1926), *Woman in Raspberry Costume Holding a Dog*, circa 1901, pastel on paper. *4.* Man Ray (American, 1890–1976), *Seguidilla*, 1919, watercolor, gouache, ink, pencil, and colored pencil on paper. *5.* Henri Matisse (French, 1869–1954), *Decorative Figure*, 1908, bronze. *6.* Piet Mondrian (Dutch, 1872–1944), *Composition with Blue and Yellow*, 1935. *7.* Vladimir Baranoff-Rossine (Russian, 1888–1942), *Capriccio Musicale*, 1913, oil and pencil on canvas, gift of Mary and Leigh Block.

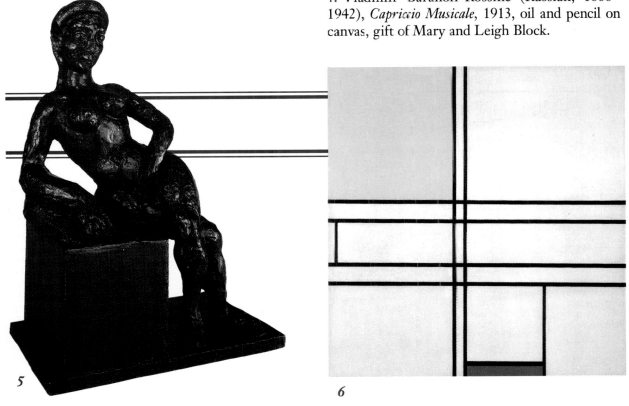

5

6

7

8

9

10

11

8. Alberto Giacometti (Swiss, 1901–1966), *Dog*, 1951 (cast, 1957), bronze. 9. Horace Pippin (American, 1888–1946), *Holy Mountain III*, 1945. 10. Frank Stella (American, b. 1936), *Quaquà! Attaccati La!*, 1985, mixed media on metal and fiberglass, museum purchase. 11. Fernand Léger (French, 1881–1955), *Nude on a Red Background*, 1927. 12. Leon Golub (American, b. 1922), *Four Black Men*, 1985, Thomas M. Evans, Jerome L. Greene, Joseph H. Hirshhorn, and Sydney and Frances Lewis Purchase Fund. 13. Claes Olden-burg (American, b. Sweden, 1929), *Geometric Mouse: Variation I, Scale A*, 1971, painted alumi-num and steel, museum purchase. 14. René Magritte (Belgian, 1898–1967), *Delusions of Gran-deur*, 1948. 15. Avigdor Arikha (Israeli, b. Ruma-nia, 1929), *The Square in June*, 1983.

13

12

14

15

Opened to the public in 1967, the Anacostia Museum was created in response to community efforts to establish a museum in the historic Anacostia section of Southeast Washington. The first of its kind in the nation, the museum provides a wide range of changing exhibitions and programs related to African-American culture and history. Research, design, and production staffs create all the exhibits. The museum also houses reference materials for use by scholars. *1.* This Sojourner Truth doll was made by Cecilia Rothman. *2.* Ed Dwight's bronze bust of Frederick Douglass honors the "Sage of Anacostia." *3.* Storytelling is one of the many popular programs offered by the museum's education department. *4. The Real McCoy* explores the contributions of African-American inventors.

# ANACOSTIA MUSEUM

1

2

3

4

Cooper-Hewitt National Museum of Design is the only U.S. museum devoted solely to historical and contemporary design. The museum's interests include all fields of design, including architecture, industrial design, landscaping, interior design, graphic arts, fashion, theater arts, and advertising. Its collection contains over 170,000 drawings, prints, decorative art objects, textiles, wall coverings, books, archival materials, and a research library. The New York City museum is housed in Andrew Carnegie's Georgian Revival mansion. *1.* Living room design, Donald Deskey, United States, 1934. *2.* "Borneo" woven and printed damask textile, Creation Baumann, Switzerland, 1987. *3.* Ceramic bowl, Elsa Rady, United States, 1984. *4.* French wallpaper dado, circa 1820, gift of Josephine Howell.

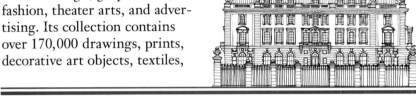

# COOPER-HEWITT NATIONAL MUSEUM OF DESIGN

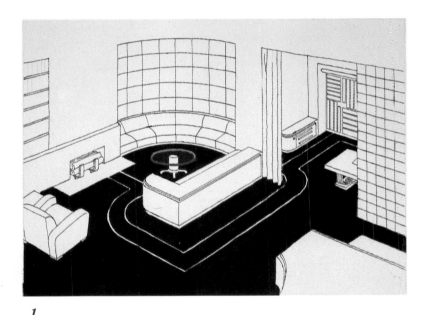

*1*

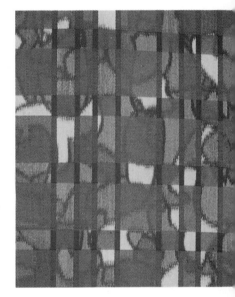

*2*

*3*

*4*

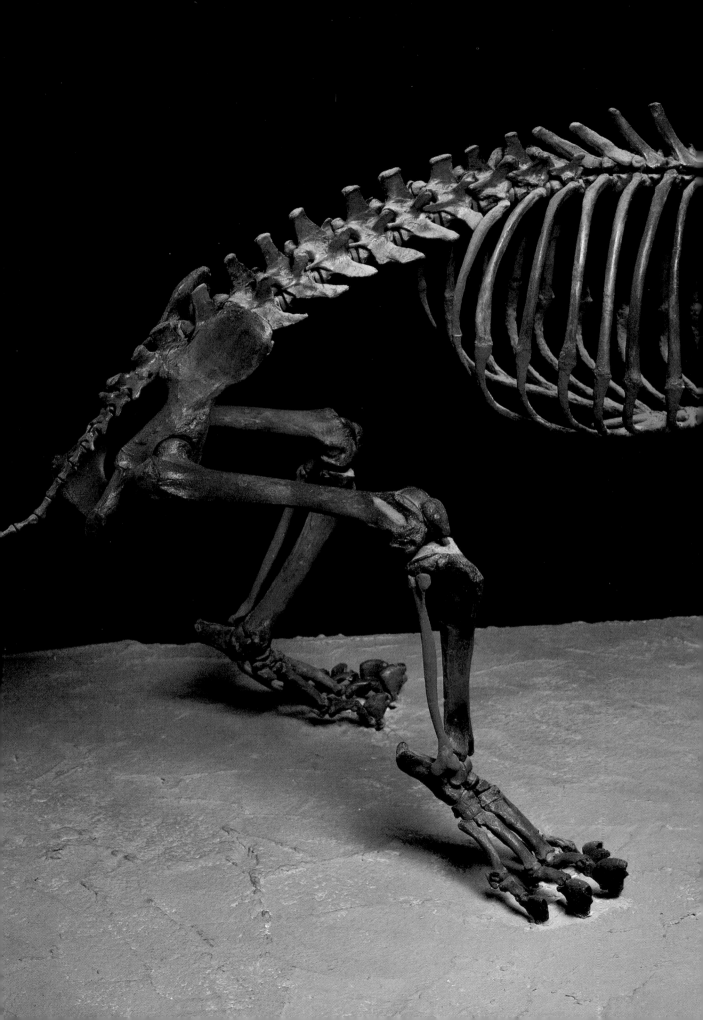

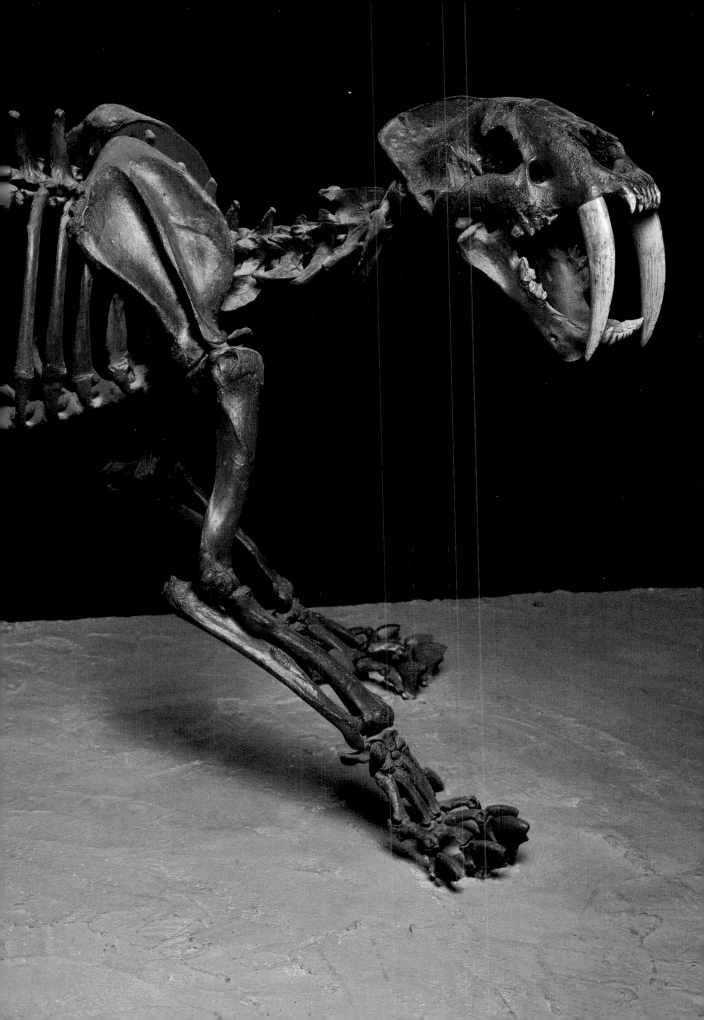

The National Museum of Natural History is the country's largest research museum, with one of the world's biggest and most valuable scientific collections. Showcased in about 20 exhibit halls, the collections include about 118 million animals, plants, fossil organisms, rocks, minerals, and cultural artifacts. *Preceding pages:* This skeleton of a sabertoothed tiger of 14,000 years ago was recovered from the sticky tar pits of Rancho La Brea, California. *1.* This is one of the nearly 10,000 different species of trilobites — marine animals that became extinct 240 million years ago. *2.* A life-size replica of *Quetzalcoatlus northropi*, a flying reptile of the Mesozoic Era, soars over the museum's dinosaur gallery. *3.* This is a skeleton of the large, plated *Stegosaurus*, which roamed the

# NATIONAL MUSEUM OF NATURAL HISTORY

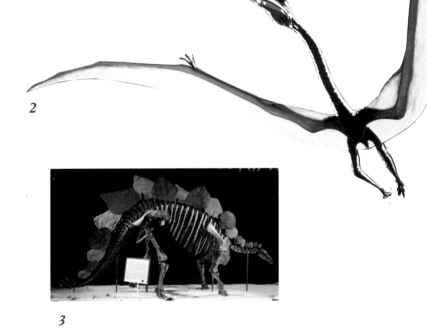

2

1

3

4

5

area that is now Colorado, Utah, and Wyoming. **4.** Ammonites, extinct relatives of squid and the nautilus, are featured fossils in this mural. **5.** A diorama of the Jurassic Period shows plant and animal life of 135 million years ago. **6.** This portion of John Gurche's *The Tower of Time*, a 27-foot mural created for the dinosaur gallery, depicts the Age of Reptiles, with the notorious *Tyrannosaurus rex* at center. **7.** The gigantic skeleton of a woolly mammoth, an extinct elephant species, is on display in the Ice Age hall. **8.** In this reconstruction of a Neanderthal burial in the Regourdou Cave, France, about 70,000 years ago, complex burial rites reflect early belief in a spiritual world. **9.** Belying its fierce appearance, *Triceratops* was a plant eater.

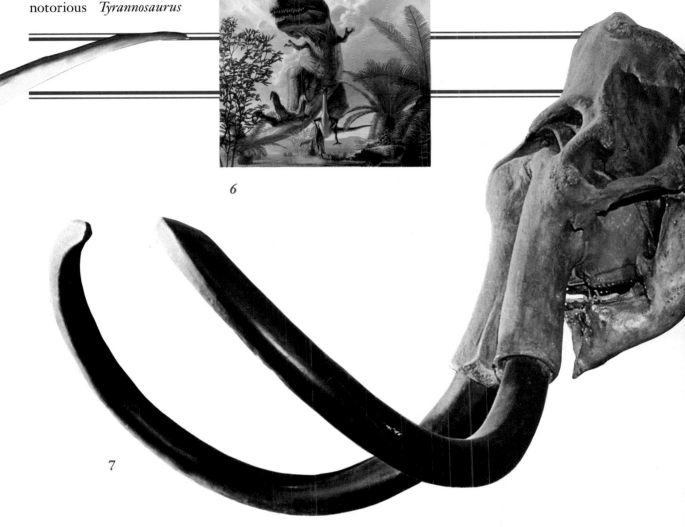

6

7

8

9

10

11

12

13

14

15

10. Weighing in at 857 pounds, this 11-foot, 1-inch Bengal tiger is believed to be the largest tiger ever taken in India. 11. The largest of penguins, the emperor penguin, and the small Adelie penguin — specimens collected by one of Admiral Richard E. Byrd's parties — are featured in this Antarctic diorama. 12. Displayed in the Sea Life hall, this blue whale is a life-size, 92-foot replica of the largest animal species on earth today. 13. Members of the Department of Paleobiology pose inside the reconstructed jaw of an extinct 4.5-million-year-old white shark — the biggest that ever lived. 14. An African bush elephant, the largest land animal on earth today, dominates the museum's rotunda. 15. The walrus, a polar marine animal, weighs as much as 3,000 pounds when full grown. 16. The white-tailed deer is one of the few large native mammals more common now than when North America was first colonized by Europeans. 17. The American alligator is an integral part of the ecosystem of swamps in the southeastern United States.

16

17

18. Ancient Egyptians embalmed this linen-wrapped cat mummy to accompany its owner into the afterlife. 19. Homer called the Trojan two-handled goblet *depas amphekephellon*, the drinking cup of royalty. 20. This grouping of African artifacts suggests the diversity and richness of African craftsmanship. 21. Representing a raven, this Kwakiutl Indian mask was made in British Columbia in 1894. 22. A diorama depicts a traditional scene of Polar Eskimo life. 23. The Zuni Indians of western New Mexico are famous for their elaborately decorated pots. 24. Navajo Indians of Arizona or New Mexico, circa 1880–1890, made this double-saddle blanket of heavy tapestry and twill. 25. This Sioux Indian eagle-feather headdress with ermine tails, horsehair, and beadwork dates roughly from 1880. 26. Constructed of 14 buffalo hides that have been laced together, this Arapaho tepee was first displayed at the Philadelphia Centennial Exposition of 1876. 27. This fringed Plains Indian war shirt was believed to provide the wearer with spiritual power.

18

19

20

21

22

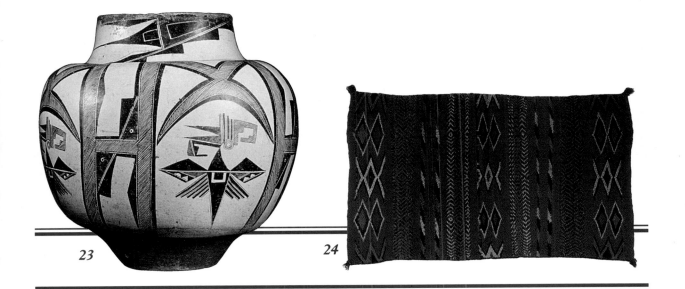

23

24

26

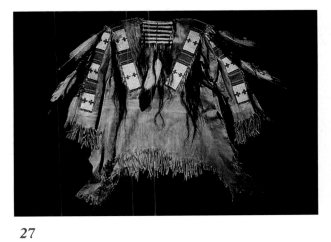

25

27

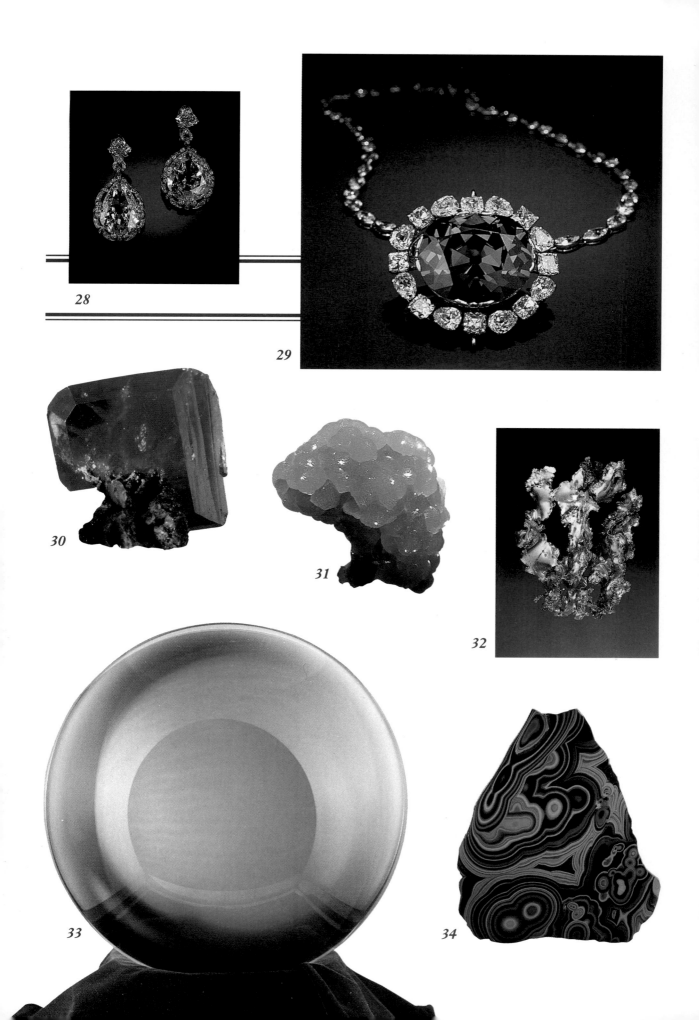

28

29

30

31

32

33

34

28. These diamond earrings are believed to have belonged to Marie Antoinette, queen of France in the 1700s. 29. The stone of the famous Hope diamond weighs 45.5 carats and is the world's largest blue diamond on public display. 30. This wulfenite sample was taken from the Red Cloud Mine in Yuma County, Arizona. 31. Smithsonite is the ore named for James Smithson, founder of the Smithsonian Institution. 32. This specimen of leaf gold, one of the finest of its kind, weighs 14.6 ounces and comes from California's Eureka Mine. 33. The Warner crystal ball, weighing 106¾ pounds, was cut from a large quartz crystal. 34. Copper carbonate creates the green color in this cross section of a piece of malachite. 35. This birdwing butterfly is from the museum's huge research collection. 36. The cone-headed grasshopper from Central America is among the residents of the Insect Zoo. 37. Cuban tree snails are treasured for their varicolored beauty. 38. A visitor in the hands-on Discovery Room investigates a stuffed crocodile.

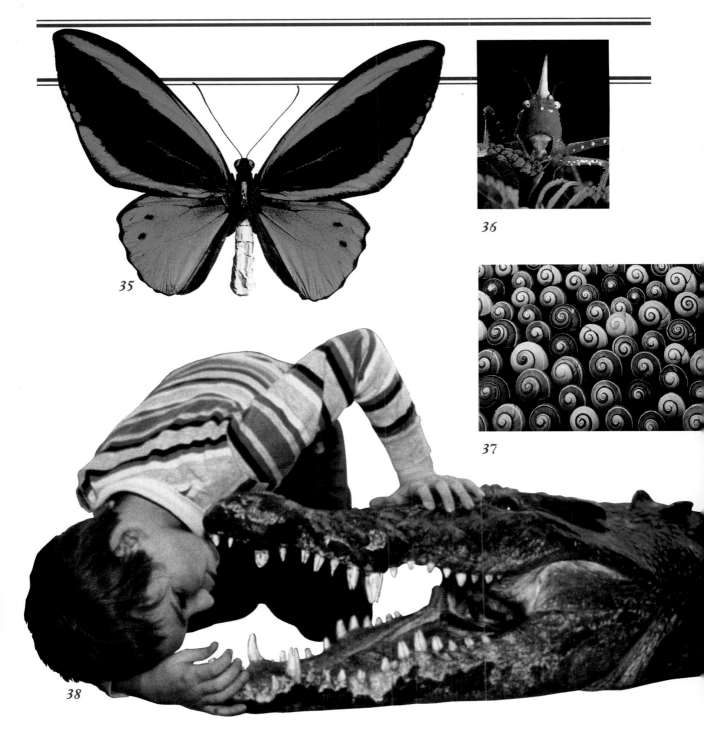

35

36

37

38

The National Zoological Park was founded in 1889 both as an educational institution and as a refuge for wildlife that was rapidly vanishing from the North American continent. Now the collection contains some 4,000 animals, representing over 400 species from all over the world and including rare and endangered species such as the giant panda. The National Zoo has pioneered research work that has led to better care of zoo animals and to the conservation of endangered and exotic species. In a current project the golden lion tamarin is being bred for reintroduction in its native habitat in Brazil. Species of plants and animals are shown together, much as they might be seen in their natural habitats; and sculpture, art, crafts, and artifacts are included wherever possible. Such arrangements promote

# NATIONAL ZOOLOGICAL PARK

1

2

3

an awareness of the relations of animals to one another, to plants, and to people. *1.* Ambika, a female Asian elephant, came to the United States in 1961 as a gift from the children of India. *2.* The bald eagle, a symbol of the United States, also symbolizes the National Zoo. *3.* The treasured giant pandas were gifts of the People's Republic of China to the people of the United States in 1972. *4.* Giraffes, the world's tallest animals, are popular Zoo animals. *5.* Two Komodo dragons, rare in zoo collections, were given to the people of the United States by the government of Indonesia. *6.* Powerful climbers and leapers, leopards require more secure enclosures than the open, moated areas of the lions and tigers. *7.* The fatty cheek pads and throat pouch identify this orangutan as an adult male; orangutans live in the wild in Sumatra and Borneo.

4

5

7

6

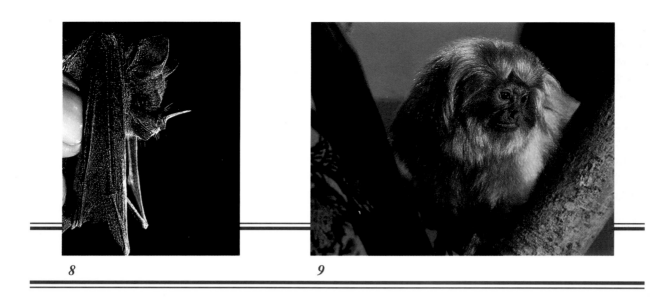

8

9

10

11

12

8. This short-tailed bat is the smallest of three species in the bat exhibit, which is specially lit for daytime viewing. 9. During warm months, free-ranging golden lion tamarins explore the trees and learn to fend for themselves before being reintroduced into the wild in Brazil. 10. Young one-horned rhinos from Nepal and northeast India are fed by their keeper. 11. In the invertebrate exhibit, a colony of leaf-cutter ants grows the fungus garden on which it also feeds. 12. The bongo is camouflaged in its native habitat in equatorial Africa but it is easily sighted on the hillside near the Bird House. 13. More than 140 species of birds, including this colorful Gouldian finch from northern Australia, live in the Bird House. 14. The wetlands exhibit supports a variety of birds, including this American merganser. 15. Emerald tree boas live near water in the Amazon basin of South America. 16. The zebra's striking stripes protect it in its natural habitat.

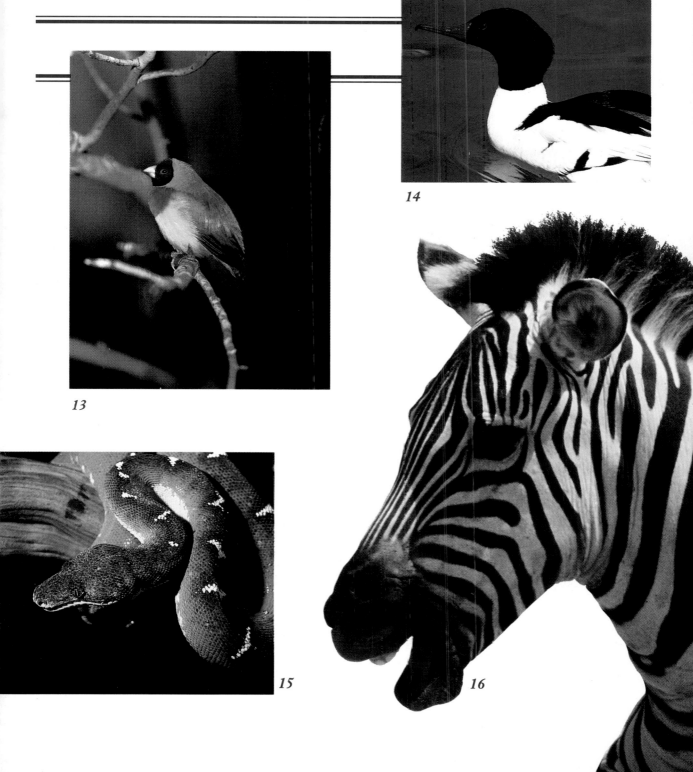

13

14

15

16

*A Picture Tour of the Smithsonian* was created by the Book Development division, Smithsonian Institution Press: Caroline Newman, Executive Editor; Paula Ballo-Dailey, Picture Editor; Ann Dargis, Copy Editor. The editors thank their colleagues at the Smithsonian who helped create this book. Smithsonian Institution Staff Photographers: Chip Clark, Jessie Cohen, Jeffrey Crespi, Harold Dorwin, Mike Fischer, Pat Harman, Al Harrell, Richard Hofmeister, Eric Long, Kim Nielsen, Dane Penland, Laurie Minor-Penland, Jeffrey Ploskonka, Lee Stalsworth, Jeff Tinsley, Rick Vargas, John Wooten. Additional photography: Ross Chapple, Ken Heinen, Robert Lautman, Charles Phillips, Rolland White.

Book Design by Meadows & Wiser
Illustrations by Kate Howe Levy

Library of Congress Cataloging-in-Publication Data
A picture tour of the Smithsonian.
    p. cm.
ISBN 0-87474-899-2
    1. Smithsonian Institution—Pictorial works. I. Smithsonian Institution.
Q11.P683 1990    069'.09753–dc20    90-9532

∞ The paper used in this publication meets the minimum requirements of the American National Standard for Permanence of Paper for Printed Library Materials Z39.48-1984.

# THE SMITHSONIAN MUSEUMS

*Smithsonian museums in Washington are open every day of the year, with the exception of December 25, and have free admission. Unless otherwise noted, hours are 10:00 A.M. to 5:30 P.M. Extended hours are determined annually.*

SMITHSONIAN INSTITUTION BUILDING (CASTLE)
1000 Jefferson Drive, S.W.
Smithsonian Information Center (9:00 A.M. to 5:30 P.M., daily), Crypt Room with Tomb of James Smithson, Administrative Offices, Woodrow Wilson International Center for Scholars

ANACOSTIA MUSEUM
1901 Fort Place, S.E.
(10:00 A.M. to 5:00 P.M.)
Museum Shop

ARTHUR M. SACKLER GALLERY
1050 Independence Avenue, S.W.
Museum Shop

ARTS AND INDUSTRIES BUILDING
Jefferson Drive at 9th Street, S.W.
Museum Shop, Discovery Theater

FREER GALLERY OF ART (REOPENS 1992)
Jefferson Drive at 12th Street, S.W.
Museum Shop

HIRSHHORN MUSEUM AND SCULPTURE GARDEN
Independence Avenue at 8th Street, S.W.
Museum Shop

NATIONAL AIR AND SPACE MUSEUM
Independence Avenue at 6th Street, S.W.
Museum Shop, Planetarium Shop, Shuttle Shop, Films and Planetarium Shows, Cafeteria

NATIONAL MUSEUM OF AFRICAN ART
950 Independence Avenue, S.W.
Museum Shop

NATIONAL MUSEUM OF AMERICAN ART
8th and G Streets, N.W.
Museum Shop, Cafeteria

NATIONAL MUSEUM OF AMERICAN HISTORY
Constitution Avenue between 12th and 14th Streets, N.W.
Museum Shop and Bookstore, Smithsonian Post Office, Cafeteria, Palm Court (ice cream parlor)

NATIONAL MUSEUM OF NATURAL HISTORY
Constitution Avenue at 10th Street, N.W.
Museum Shop, Cafeteria, Smithsonian Associates' Dining Room, Discovery Room, Naturalist Center, Evans Gallery

NATIONAL PORTRAIT GALLERY
8th and F Streets, N.W.
Museum Shop, Cafeteria

NATIONAL ZOOLOGICAL PARK
Entrances: Connecticut Avenue, N.W. (3000 block between Cathedral Avenue and Devonshire Place); Harvard Street and Adams Mill Road intersection; Beach Drive in Rock Creek Park
*Winter hours:*
Grounds: 8:00 A.M. to 6:00 P.M.
Buildings: 9:00 A.M. to 4:30 P.M.
*Summer hours:*
Grounds: 8:00 A.M. to 8:00 P.M.
Buildings: 9:00 A.M. to 6:00 P.M.
Gift Shop, Parking Facilities, Food and Picnic Facilities

RENWICK GALLERY OF THE NATIONAL MUSEUM OF AMERICAN ART
Pennsylvania Avenue at 17th Street
Museum Shop

S. DILLON RIPLEY CENTER
1100 Jefferson Drive, S.W.
International Gallery

*In New York City*
COOPER-HEWITT NATIONAL MUSEUM OF DESIGN
2 East 91st Street, New York, New York
Tuesday, 10:00 A.M. to 9:00 P.M. (free after 5 P.M.); Wednesday through Saturday, 10:00 A.M. to 5:00 P.M.; Sunday, noon to 5:00 P.M.; closed Monday and major holidays. Museum Shop. Admission charged.

*The Smithsonian facilities also include:*
Archives of American Art
Conservation and Research Center of the National Zoo
Paul E. Garber Preservation, Restoration, and Storage Facility
Smithsonian Astrophysical Observatory
Smithsonian Environmental Research Center
Smithsonian Marine Station at Link Port
Smithsonian Tropical Research Institute